I'm Bad at Poems

I'm Bad at Poems

Here's the Proof

A collection of sixty-three poems

by

Martin Miller-Yianni

Cover photograph credit:
Photograph by Joshua Fuller
Obtained from Unsplash.com

Illustration photograph credit:
Photograph by J. R. Korpa
Obtained from Unsplash.com

Publisher: M P Miller-Yianni, Yambol, Bulgaria.

Published: May 2023 (1st Edition)

ISBN 978-619-92494-2-0 (paperback)

A catalogue record for this book is available from:

The National Register of Published Books in Bulgaria
bulevard 'Vasil Levski' 88,
1504 Sofia,
Bulgaria

Forward

"I'm Bad at Poems" is an anthology born during the spring of 2022 until late spring of 2023, composed by an ambitious poet who, while confined to a hospital bed, fearlessly explores the uncharted realms of imagination. It candidly acknowledges their initial insecurities, capturing the essence of a debutant poet, doubting their abilities and embracing vulnerability. The collection defies conventions, allowing creativity to wander freely.

Within its pages, readers embark on a captivating journey into the world of random thoughts and emotions. Unfettered by structures or thematic constraints, the poems forge deep connections with themes of love, loss, self-discovery, nature, dreams, and the human condition. Imperfections are celebrated, and the act of writing poems is seen as a courageous voyage of self-expression.

The poetry's content challenges norms, celebrating the chaos and randomness in the poet's mind, reminding us of the countless possibilities within the realms of poetry. The collection is not only a source of creativity but also serves as therapy for the poet during his hospital stay, allowing him to escape the boredom of four walls and immerse themselves in the world of imagination through writing.

Prepare to be charmed by the unfiltered voice of the author and their readiness to embrace the uncertainties of poetic talent. Each poem is a piece of the author's soul, inviting readers on a journey of self-discovery.

Enter into this poetic adventure and delve into the profound and ordinary. Allow the uncompromising honesty and boundless creativity of the poetic collection to captivate you, leaving you inspired and moved by the raw essence of human expression.

***

Table of Contents

1 - THE OCEAN'S SONG

In the realm of the sea, a ballad unfolds,
A sestina of waves, a chant so sublime,
As the ebb and flow resonate, tales untold,
Harmonies of nature transcending time.

Each crest and trough, a stanza they portray,
A symphony unbound, the ocean's decree,
Refrains of salty breeze, melodies sway,
In the cadence of tides, a captivating plea.

The first wave emerges, a vibrant note anew,
A refrain that echoes, in the depths so deep,
With each swell and surge, the melody grew,
Enchanting the soul, a lullaby to keep.

And as the ocean's choir surges and subsides,
A chorus of whispers, an ancient refrain,
An orchestral crescendo, where passion resides,
In this aquatic ballet, its beauty unrestrained.

Upon the shore we stand, a witness so blessed,
Immersed in the rhapsody of nature's embrace,
In awe of the power, where land and sea coalesce,
Enveloped by the symphony, our spirits find solace.

For the ocean's song, a tale so profound,
Transcends the realm of mere mortal domain,
In the sestina of waves, its secrets unbound,
A testament to life's eternal refrain.

As we heed its call, our souls start to soar,
Bound to the rhythm, a harmonious blend,
In the ocean's song, forever we'll adore,
A melody resounding, that shall never end.

*****

2 - THE MOUNTAIN'S MAJESTY

Behold the mountain's majesty so grand,
A towering peak, a symbol of command.
When sun does set, and stars expand their light,
The mountain's splendour fills the realm of sight.

Each rock, a testament to strength profound,
Each peak, a throne where solace can be found.
Though solitude may linger in this space,
Nature's embrace ensures our hearts find grace.

As we behold the mountain's wondrous might,
A vibrant pulse ignites within the night.
For nature's beauty, in its purest form,
Stirs awe and wonder, feelings to transform.

Oh, let us revel in this breath-taking view,
The mountain's majesty, forever true.

*****

3 - The Sky's Canvas

In the sky up above, a masterpiece unfolds,
A canvas of colours, a sight to behold.
As the sun starts to set, and the stars start to shine,
The sky's canvas comes to life, a moment so divine.

Each cloud is a brush stroke, each hue is a shade,
As the sky paints its picture, we feel unafraid.
For in this moment, a connection is made,
A bond with nature that will never fade.

We gaze upon the canvas, as night takes its hold,
And we feel a sense of light, that warms us like gold.
For the beauty of nature, in its wondrous delight,
Fills us with hope, and a joy that takes flight.

The sky's canvas, a masterpiece so fine,
A moment to define, a moment that's divine.
As the stars align, and the colours combine,
We're reminded of nature's beauty, that will forever shine.

*****

4 - ABOUT POEMS

Poems are magic woven in words,
A tapestry of thoughts, feelings and chords.
They can make you laugh, or cry, or dream,
And transport you to places you've never seen.

Some poems are like a gentle breeze,
Whispering secrets through the trees.
Others are a raging storm,
Powerful and fierce, they transform.

Poems are windows to the soul,
A mirror reflecting life's hidden goal.
They capture the essence of the human heart,
And inspire us to create our own art.

From haikus to sonnets, ballads to free verse,
Poems come in many forms, each with a unique force.
They remind us that language is a gift,
And that the power of words can give us a lift.

So let us cherish these jewels of expression,
For they offer us endless inspiration.
May we always find joy in the poetry of life,
And keep the magic of words alive.

*****

5 - THE DELIGHTS OF YOGHURT

Creamy and cool, a delight so pure,
Yoghurt, a treat, a taste to endure.
With every spoonful, probiotics embrace,
Gut's gratitude, a bountiful embrace.

Digestion aided, bowels find ease,
Yoghurt, the saviour, hungers appease.
Protein and calcium, it graciously imparts,
Strengthens bones, muscles, vital parts.

Low in calories, fat it defies,
Yoghurt, ally of healthy choices, arise.
Versatile it stands, in myriad arrays,
Smoothies, dips, a symphony of praise.

With fruit and honey, or spices to blend,
Yoghurt's magic, a journey without end.
When hunger calls, and snacks distract,
Yoghurt's the answer, no turning back.

For wellness it bestows, a resounding cry,
Yoghurt, the food that satisfies, oh my!

*****

6 - WHY WAR?

Oh war, you are a senseless game of strife,
Where weapons clash and lives are lost in vain,
With fathers, brothers, sons prepared for life,
But doomed to perish on the battlefield plain.

Divided nations, drawn by borders' lines,
The reasons for their battles long forgot,
Their once-friends now seen as foes with designs,
Lives shattered, futures gone, with peace unsought.

Families torn, with cities laid to waste,
Young children left alone, without employ,
While bullets fly and bombs explode with haste,
And peaceful lives are forever destroyed.

The cost of war is never worth the gain,
A cycle of violence that repeats again.

Let us forsake this madness and unite,
Strive for peace, and put an end to this blight.

*****

7 - LONELINESS

Loneliness, a constant companion,
A shadow that follows without relent,
A silence that echoes in every canyon,
A weight that bears down with intent.

It creeps in slowly like a thief,
Stealing the joy from every day,
Leaving behind a sense of grief,
A feeling that never goes away.

It's an ache that fills the soul,
A longing for something undefined,
An emptiness that takes its toll,
A darkness that clouds the mind.

The world seems to move on without us,
As we sit alone in our despair,
Yearning for just a bit of fuss,
Longing for someone who might care.

But in the midst of this endless night,
We must remember we're not alone,
For even in the darkest plight,
A glimmer of hope can still be shown.

So let us reach out to one another,
To break the chains of isolation,
And find solace in the embrace of another,
And mend our hearts with connection.

*****

8 - THE PIG (NATO MEMBER) AND THE WOLF

In a green field, a joyful pig resided,
With a curly tail and a life undivided.
But danger approached, a wolf drew near,
Trembling with fear, the pig shed a tear.

Thunder roared, NATO allies arrived,
To protect the pig, valiant and unified.
With unwavering courage, they faced the beast,
Defending the innocent, their mission increased.

Mighty jets soared and tanks rolled in,
NATO's strength showing evil can't win.
The wolf slinked away, defeated and dismayed,
Knowing NATO's might had come to aid.

Grateful, the pig rejoiced, forever in debt,
NATO's unity, a symbol we won't forget.
When darkness descends, they stand so strong,
Protecting the vulnerable, righting the wrong.

Let's remember their intervention so grand,
NATO's presence, a force that expands.
In fields of green, gratitude shall bloom,
For NATO's rescue dispelling all gloom.

*****

9 - I'm a Bad at Poems

Here I sit, pen in hand, with a soul that yearns,
Words swirling in the vast expanse, my spirit burns.
But as I try to capture thoughts, to make them grand,
My efforts fall flat, slipping through my trembling hand.

Oh, I know, I am bad at poems, that much is clear to see,
My verses lack rhythm and rhyme, escaping me.
I struggle to mould my words into a crafted form,
To weave a tapestry of beauty, to weather life's storm.

My metaphors feel stale, trite, devoid of flair,
My similes fail to ignite, leaving me in despair.
The imagery I conjure lacks that vibrant might,
To seize the reader's sight, to make their hearts take flight.

I envy those whose words flow like a river's thrill,
Whose verses dance and sing, with a masterful skill.
But here I am, stumbling, tripping over lines,
A struggling poet, searching for words that truly shine.

Still pressing on, with every pen stroke I take,
Hoping that someday, somehow, my voice will awake.
For within me lies a passion, a fire burning bright,
And though my verses stumble, they yearn to ignite.

So, I continue to pour my heart onto the page,
Knowing that improvement comes with each engaged stage.
Though tonight I may be a bad at poems, lost in my plight,
Tomorrow, I'll rise again, armed with renewed insight.

With each line, I strive to capture life's divine grace,
To paint emotions, in words, find a sacred space.
For it is the love of creation that keeps me strong,
With each imperfect verse, I journey towards where I belong.

Me and my struggling pen, we shall persist, hand in hand,
Navigating the vast ocean of thoughts, we'll expand.
In the depths of our imperfections, a truth does lie,
That the beauty of the journey is to never cease to try.

Hopefully, together we'll march forward, through darkness and light,
In pursuit of that elusive harmony, both fierce and bright.
No longer am I bad at poems, but a poet learning to be,
With hope as my compass, I'll uncover the poet within me.

*****

Love, love, why must you be
So complicated, so hard to see
We hold onto memories of what once was
And wonder why we couldn't make it last

So complicated, so hard to see
We chase after you with all our might
And wonder why we couldn't make it last
You make us feel alive, then leave us in vain

We chase after you with all our might
We give our hearts, our souls, our all
You make us feel alive, then leave us in vain
But sometimes love can make us fall

We give our hearts, our souls, our all
We search and search for that perfect fit
But sometimes love can make us fall
Yet still we seek you out, time and time again

We search and search for that perfect fit
We hold onto memories of what once was
Yet still we seek you out, time and time again
For the hope that one day we'll find

We hold onto memories of what once was
We give our hearts, our souls, our all
For the hope that one day we'll find
The love that's true, the love that's kind

We give our hearts, our souls, our all
Love, oh love, why must you be
The love that's true, the love that's kind
Love, oh love, why must you be

*****

20

11 - INSULT WITHOUT FOUNDATION

Oh, how harsh and cruel your words,
Cut through the air like sharpened swords,
"Why are you rubbish?" you inquire,
But I don't stoke the fiery ire.

"You're good for nothing," you now declare,
But your reasoning, you fail to share,
"You're fit for nothing," you searingly repeat,
But your insults, they just sound like deceit.

And then you call me "scum brain,"
My worth and value, you disdain,
But tell me, friend, how can it be true,
That I'm worthless, with nothing to do?

Perhaps you're blinded by anger and hate,
Or jealousy that I cannot abate,
But still, I ask, please substantiate,
Your claims of my worthlessness and fate.

For I refuse to believe your baseless words,
I know I have value, like singing birds,
And though you may try to bring me down,
I'll rise above, and wear my crown.

So go ahead, insult and deride,
But know that I will not subside,
I am not rubbish, I am not scum,
I am a person, and my worth cannot be undone.

*****

12 - MADE TO MEASURE

Measures, measures, they matter so much,
Inches and centimetres, and such and such.
How long is it? We need to know,
For if it's too short, it won't go.
How wide does it measure, won't fit without knowing,
A fraction too big, and we'll be left moaning.
We measure and measure, to get it just right,
Hoping our estimation won't cause us a fight.

How much liquid to fill it? To the brim is essential,
Too little or too much, and it's consequential.
We measure with care, and pour with precision,
To ensure we don't create a liquid collision.
How much does it weigh? Don't want to break my back,
A measurement error, could cause a painful attack.
We lift and we heave, with a careful approach,
To make sure we don't strain, or cause any reproach.

How tall is she? She has to be shorter than me,
A measurement that's wrong, and it's plain to see.
We stand back-to-back, and we check our height,
To make sure we don't cause any height fright.
How much time do you have? Tell me honestly,
A measurement we can't ignore, or treat nonchalantly.
We check our clock, and plan our day,
To ensure we don't waste any precious time away.

Measures, measures, guessing never good enough,
We strive for accuracy, and measurements that are tough.
We measure and measure, to get it just right,
So, we can rest easy, and sleep soundly at night.

*****

13 - THE ROSE

The rose's beauty fades away,
Each petal drops, memories stay,
Lessons taught within its fleeting days,
Cherishing moments, life's vibrant haze,
Time's passage, an impermanent phase.

Love and live, make every second count,
Petals fall, but memories amount,
Life, like a rose, transient in its mount,
Cherished moments, stories to recount,
In faded beauty, hope's promise will sprout.

Amidst dark times, hope we'll still embrace,
The dormant rose, a symbol of grace,
Promising better days, a hopeful trace,
Life's brevity, a reason to chase,
Memories crafted, leaving a lasting trace.

Let us embrace life's ephemeral flow,
Moments cherished, like petals aglow,
In the end, it's the memories we sow,
Through blooming roses, love's essence will show,
Forever imprinted, even when we must go.

*****

14 - BLOODY POEMS - THEY DO MY HEAD IN

Bloody poems they do my head in,
I can't seem to catch their meaning,
Words swirl around in my mind,
But their significance, I can't find.

I try to read them, line by line,
But they always seem to be so divine,
So abstract, so deep and obscure,
Like a puzzle that I can't procure.

I wonder if the poets themselves,
Ever found meaning in their wealth,
Of metaphors, similes, and rhymes,
That seem to me like pointless chimes.

Perhaps they saw something I can't,
A message in the rhythm and chant,
A secret code that only they knew,
But to me, it's just a jumbled hue.

I envy those who appreciate,
The beauty of the poet's slate,
Who see beyond the words and phrases,
And understand the hidden traces.

But alas, I am not one of those,
And so, bloody poems do my head in,
I'll keep on trying, nonetheless,
Hoping one day, I'll find success.

*****

15 - I Don't Want To Solve Puzzles

I don't want to solve puzzles,
The weight of it all just feels like a muzzle,
My brain feels foggy, my thoughts are unclear,
I just want to shut down and hide from here,
But as I sit and let my mind drift away,
I know deep down that I cannot stay.

For life is a puzzle that we must solve,
And challenges are what help us evolve,
The joy of solving a problem is sweet,
It's a feeling that simply can't be beat,
To see the pieces all fit into place,
Is a triumph that puts a smile on your face.

Never give up or throw in the towel,
Let's put on our thinking caps and give it a scowl,
For the puzzles we face may seem daunting and tough,
But with a little perseverance, we'll rise above,
The answers may not come right away,
We may stumble and fall along the way.

But as we keep on trying and never give in,
We'll find a solution and we'll win,
So, let's not shy away from thinking or puzzles,
For they are the keys to unlocking life's struggles,
Embrace the challenge, let your mind take flight,
And soon you'll see the world in a brand-new light.

*****

16 - HATE

In a world so interconnected,
We find ourselves so disconnected,
Fuelled by anger, resentment and fear,
Our hearts have hardened, it's crystal clear,
We hate without a second thought,
Judging others for what they've wrought,
Blaming them for all our strife,
As if they were the cause of our life.

Social media, a breeding ground,
For hate to spread and be found,
Trolls and bots, all around,
Filling our feeds with a deafening sound.

Our differences, once a source of strength,
Now divide us, to an unprecedented length,
Race, religion, politics and more,
All used to create an invisible war.

We forget that we're all human,
And that love is the ultimate solution,
Instead, we choose to hate and fight,
In a world that should be filled with light,
Let us break free from this cycle,
And open our hearts, to love and smile,
For only then, can we truly see,
That we're all part of one big family.

Let us set aside our biases and fears,
And wipe away our bitter tears,
For only then, can we truly thrive,
And create a world where love is alive.

We must learn to celebrate our diversity,
And cherish our unique complexity,
For it is our differences that make us strong,
And give us the ability to right the wrong.

Let us choose compassion over judgment,
And forgiveness over resentment,
For only then, can we truly heal,
And create a world where love can be real,
Let us build bridges instead of walls,
And answer hate with love, when it calls,
For it is only through love that we can win,
And create a world that's free from sin.

So let us start a revolution of love,
And rise above, the hate that's been shoved,
Into our hearts and into our minds,
And leave it all behind.

We are all brothers and sisters,
Living under the same stars and twisters,
In this beautiful world we call home,
Let us not forget, we are never alone.

*****

17 - My Dog

All for the love of my Black Labrador friend,
I used to wake up each morning with a brisk set,
With a wag of his tail, he couldn't hide,
By my side, he was always in stride.

He used to greet me with a lick like a kiss,
The warmth and love that he brought, I never miss,
Our bond was one of life's great things,
His presence, to my heart, it forever clings.

We used to walk the canal, side by side,
My companion, my buddy and also my guide,
He used to lead me to the fields to run,
And have some fun even with no sun.

In the garden, my dog used to play with glee,
Running and jumping, he was always carefree,
Proud of the joy my best friend brought in,
I used to sit and watch with a satisfied grin.

All for the love of my Black Labrador friend,
I was blessed to have that bond 'till the end,
His paw prints remain in my heart,
And memories of Widget will never depart.

*****

18 - Morning Dew

Morning dew, a glistening sight
A moment of peace, a moment of might
As the world awakens to a new light
Nature's beauty is in full flight

Each blade of grass, each petal of a flower
Is adorned with droplets, a magical power
A symbol of life, of nature's shower
Of something greater, of a higher tower

And as the day unfolds, the dew will dry
But for a moment, we can't deny
The beauty of nature, the reason why
We wake up each morning, under a clear sky.

*****

19 - POLITICIANS

In grand halls of power, they stand so tall,
With eloquent speeches and grandiose calls,
Promising change and a brighter tomorrow,
But their words ring hollow, filled with only sorrow.
They bicker and fight like children at play,
Their egos so big, they get in the way,
Of progress and action, of unity and peace,
Their partisan agendas never seem to cease.

They promise the world, but deliver so little,
Their rhetoric grand, but their actions so brittle,
They spin and they weave, but the truth is clear,
Their promises are empty, their words insincere.

They dance to the tune of their corporate masters,
Their pockets lined with gold, they forget the disasters,
That the people they serve, face every day,
Their struggles ignored, as the politicians play.

The people cry out, but their voices are lost,
In the endless noise of politicians, at any cost,
To stay in power and maintain their fame,
Their priorities twisted; their morals so lame.
Oh, how futile these politicians are,
As they sit in their thrones, so very far,
From the people they serve, their voices so small,
Their hopes and dreams crushed, by politicians' brawl.

It's time for a change, a new way to lead,
With honesty and integrity, a new seed,
Of hope and compassion, of courage and grace,
A leader who listens, with an open face.

Let's rise up, and demand a better way,
For the future we seek, for a brighter day,
Let's show the politicians, that we are strong,
That together we can right the wrong.

For in the end, it's not the politicians who win,
But the people who rise up, and overcome the sin,
Of greed and corruption, of lies and deceit,
With hope in their hearts, and a new world to meet.

*****

20 - Socialists? Just a Dream

In a world that seems so broken and unfair,
Where the rich keep getting richer, and the poor left to despair,
Where corporate greed and political corruption reign,
A true socialist system feels like a hope so rare.

Imagine a world where the wealth is shared,
Where no one is left hungry or without care,
Where education and healthcare are free for all,
And everyone has a fair chance to rise and stand tall.

No more would we see the exploitation of the working class,
Or the hoarding of resources by the privileged few,
For in a true socialist system, the power is with the people,
And the needs of the many come before the interests of the few.

The community would be the cornerstone of society,
With cooperation and solidarity as our guiding light,
We would work together towards a common goal,
And strive for the greater good with all our might.

Gone would be the days of corporate greed and excess,
Or the politicians who serve only their own interests,
For in a true socialist system, the power is with the people,
And every voice is heard and every need is met.

Yes, a true socialist system may seem like a dream,
But it is a dream worth striving for,
For a world built on cooperation, equality, and care,
Is a world worth fighting for evermore.

In the political realm, there are those who claim
To be socialist, with a socialist name,
Yet their actions speak louder than words,
And their rhetoric may be nothing but a facade.

For there are wolves in sheep's clothing, it seems,
Who use socialist language to propagate their schemes,
And while they claim to fight for the working class,
Their true loyalties lie with the wealthy and powerful brass.

They may speak of justice and equality,
But their actions show a different reality,
Where the interests of the few takes centre stage,
And the working class is left to struggle and wage.

Yet we must not let these wolves go unseen,
For they threaten to shatter our socialist dream,
And the fight for justice and equality,
Must continue with unwavering tenacity.

Let us hold all politicians accountable,
And demand that they serve the people, not the unaccountable,
For true socialism is not just words on a page,
But a system that empowers the working class, and paves the way to a new
age.

Let us reject the wolves in sheep's clothing,
And instead work towards a world more loving,
Where justice and equality reign supreme,
And the true power lies with the people, and not just a dream.

*****

21 - A Magical World

Amidst green fields, where rolling hills arise,
A hidden realm, unseen by mortal sight,
A world of magic, wonder, and surprise.

Enchanting melodies fill the air, light,
Whispering secrets carried on the breeze,
As stars adorn the sky, their celestial might.

Within the forests, vibrant life's at ease,
Creatures dancing with grace beneath the trees,
The leaves rustling with an ethereal tease.

Gentle rivers murmur as they flow free,
Meandering through the land's enchanting face,
Reflecting the beauty of sky and sea.

Here, magic thrives, infusing every space,
A tranquil realm where peace forever reigns,
And kindness illuminates every trace.

The people, wise and kind, embrace these plains,
Their voices harmonize, a joyful ring,
Uniting like birds soaring in refrains.

Their homes exude warmth, hearth fires that sing,
And in their eyes, a sparkle shines so bright,
Like stars emerging after storm clouds swing.
This world, resplendent in its sheer delight,
Where dreams transpire and stars guide the way,
A sanctuary where troubles take flight.

In this realm, life unfolds, a precious ray,
Each cherished day, a gift of love's embrace,
For love and memories endure, they say.

So let us bask in this enchanted space,
Where the world weaves its magic tale,
And in our hearts, find solace and embrace.

*****

22 - Mysterious Witchcraft

In the dark of night when the moon is bright,
And the wind whispers secrets with all its might,
There is a magic that stirs in the air,
A power that only witches dare to dare.

With potions and spells and a broomstick ride,
They cast their enchantments with the tide,
Their cauldrons bubble and their candles flicker,
As they weave their spells with a wicked snicker.

From the roots of herbs to the wings of bats,
They gather their ingredients for their witchy acts,
With a wave of their wand and a cackle of glee,
They brew up a potion for all to see.

They call upon the spirits of the earth and sky,
To guide their magic as they fly,
Through the forests and over the seas,
They harness the power of the ancient trees.

With a flick of their finger and a twirl of their dress,
They conjure up spells with their mystical finesse,
They dance in circles and chant in rhyme,
As they harness the energy of the divine.

With a wink of their eye and a twist of their tongue,
They cast their spells till the morning sun,
And when the day breaks and the night is done,
They vanish into thin air, with their magic won.

For witchcraft is a mystery, a power untold,
A force of nature that cannot be controlled,
It's a magic that lies within us all,
A reminder that we are never truly small.

*****

23 - FOR THE LOVE OF MUSIC

In opulent halls aglow with the warm hue of golden light,
The atmosphere is steeped in quietude, as the audience is polite,
As the mellifluous notes of classical music pour forth,
Enveloping all in an ethereal aura, taking them on a journey to the north.

The violins' strings sing, the cellos' strings weep,
The timpani's resounding booms, the flutes' trills leap,
Each instrument's voice resonates, merging in a symphonic blaze,
Stirring up emotions and setting souls ablaze.

The melodies soar, the harmonies intertwine,
In a timeless dance of enchanting design,
A spellbinding beauty that stirs the soul within,
And lingers long after the music has ceased to spin.

The love of classical music is a flame that burns eternal,
An unquenchable passion that's forever infernal,
From Bach to Beethoven, Mozart to Brahms,
Its allure remains, a timeless anthem.

It speaks to the heart in a language universal,
Elevating one's spirits to a realm celestial,
That defies words and transcends the constraints of time,
A divine inspiration, a symphony sublime.

The love of classical music is a journey,
An odyssey that's both challenging and merry,
It takes the listener to uncharted lands,
And opens up a world that's intricate and grand.

So let the music fill your heart and mind,
And take you on a journey of a kind,
That only the love of classical music can provide,
And in its enchanting magic, let your soul abide.

*****

In the depths of the ocean blue,
Where the light fades to darkness too,
A world of creatures roams the deep,
In an endless, wondrous leap.

Among them, the fish stand out,
A rainbow of colours, there's no doubt,
Their scales, their fins, their tails,
In an underwater ballet, they sail.

From the speedy sailfish to the clownfish small,
Each one unique, their beauty enthrals,
In schools they swim, synchronised,
A stunning display, harmonised.

But beyond the beauty and the grace,
Lies a darker, sadder place,
Where human hands have reached the seas,
And wrought destruction with careless ease.

The nets, the hooks, the trawling gear,
Tear apart the reefs, the homes, the clear,
And every fish that swims the blue,
Is caught and killed, their fate is true.

Yet still, amidst the human strife,
A glimmer of hope can come to life,
If we remember to act with care,
And to the oceans show repair.

We must protect the coral reefs,
And all the creatures that it keeps,
For if we fail, the fish will go,
And the seas, their beauty, will no longer show.

So let us pledge to change our ways,
And protect the oceans for all our days,
So that the fish may swim and thrive,
And their beauty, in our hearts, will survive.

*****

We see it every day,
In the news and on the streets,
The greed that's causing pain,
And making life so bleak.

The power-hungry few,
Who care not for the rest,
Are driven by a lust,
That leaves us all oppressed.

They exploit our labour,
For their own selfish gain,
While they bask in their riches,
We're left with nothing but pain.

The divide grows ever wider,
As they take more and more,
While those who are struggling,
Are left out in the cold.

Our world is full of suffering,
As greed runs rampant still,
And those who are in power,
Only serve their own will.

They use their influence,
To manipulate the system,
To keep us in the dark,
And keep us from wisdom.

But we will not be silenced,
We will not be ignored,
For the future of our world,
Is something to be adored.

We'll stand up to the greed,
And fight for what is right,
Until the world we live in,
Is no longer such a blight.

For we know in our hearts,
That the world can be fair,
If we come together,
And show we truly care.

We'll fight for our planet,
For our children and more,
And we'll put an end to greed,
So, the world can restore.

So let us unite,
And stand tall and strong,
For a world without greed,
Is where we truly belong.

*****

26 - FOREST'S WHISPERS

Amidst the forest's whispers, a voice so pure and clear
As the leaves rustle and the birds chirp, it draws near
We feel connected to this natural lure
For nature's beauty is a remedy, a cure

Each tree stands tall, a guardian in its place
Each bush and flower, a friend to embrace
As we walk amidst this wonderland, we understand
The value of nature, the need to lend a hand

The beauty of this place is more than what meets the eye
It's a world of balance, a harmony that never dies
The forest's whispers speak of something greater, something to trust
And in this moment, we must listen, for our ways to adjust

Let the trees be our guides, and the wind our friend
Let the forest be our sanctuary, a place to mend
For in this peaceful realm, we find solace and peace
And in its embrace, our hearts find release

So let us honour this treasure, this natural beauty
Let us cherish and protect it, our sacred duty
For the forest's whispers are a reminder to all
To live in harmony with nature, lest we fall.

*****

27 - JUST TEA (NO MILK)

In the realm of tea, an ode shall I weave,
A sestina of black tea, pure and true,
Where verses dance with rhythm and belief,
Unveiling tales of flavours, rich and new.
Milk's union with tea, a solemn crime,
Defying nature's law, against the brew's prime.

The essence, strong, emboldens hearts so brave,
As darkness swirls within each fragrant cup.
Black tea, an elixir, untamed and grave,
A symphony of taste that wakes us up.
Yet milk intrudes, a meddler to the core,
Weakening brew's spirit, forevermore.

Oh, sacrilege! The tea lover's despair,
To witness milk's betrayal, black tea's plight.
A marriage ill-conceived, beyond repair,
An offense that dulls the palate's delight.
Let not the milk entwine with tea's embrace,
Preserve the purity, keep sacred space.

For black tea's journey is a solo quest,
To steep in solitude, unhindered, free.
No milky haze should stain its noble crest,
Embrace its strength, unadulterated spree.
In unity with leaves, it finds its voice,
An elixir deserving our utmost choice.

A sin it is, to mar this sacred drink,
A practice shunned, for harmony's demand.
Let not the taint of milk lead us to brink,
But revel in black tea, forever grand.
So, raise your cups, pure black tea we adore,
In reverence we sip, forevermore.

*****

28 - MY BODY ACHES

My body aches, it's not hard to explain
A constant pain, a daily refrain
It haunts me like a ghostly chain
That never lets go, that causes strain

I try to hide it, put on a smile
But inside I'm hurting all the while
It's hard to cope with this trial
To find relief, to reconcile

I've tried every cure, every pill
But nothing seems to help, it's still
A burden I must bear, until
I find a way to break this drill

So, I soldier on, day by day
Through the pain that won't go away
I keep pushing, hoping to find a way
To ease the hurt, to brighten the grey

And though it's tough, I won't give in
I'll keep fighting until I win
For even in the midst of this din
I know there's hope, a chance to begin

So, I'll keep walking, step by step
Through the pain, with each breath
Until the day when I can forget
The constant pain, the daily threat

*****

29 - SADNESS

Tears fall like raindrops
As sadness fills my heart
The weight of the world
Pulls me down, tears me apart
I long for happiness
To chase away the pain
But it eludes me still
Leaving only this refrain
Of sorrow and despair
That fills my every thought
Oh, how I wish for solace
From this sadness I have caught.

I'm lost in a sea of sadness
With no way to find the shore
The waves of grief keep crashing
And I can't take it anymore
My heart is heavy with sorrow
And my mind is filled with pain
I wish that I could escape it
But it seems to be my only refrain
Oh, how I long for a reprieve
From this never-ending sadness
But until it passes, I'll stay adrift
In this sea of utter madness.

My heart is filled with sorrow
And my soul is filled with grief
The weight of the world on my shoulders
Is almost too much to bear, like a thief
Stealing away my joy and peace
Leaving only sadness in its place

I try to fight it, but it's so strong
That I'm left with tears on my face
Oh, how I wish that I could escape
This pain that grips my heart
But until it subsides, I'll stay here
And let my sadness play its part.

The world feels grey and lifeless
As sadness fills my heart
I try to find a ray of hope
But it seems that it's all fallen apart
My mind is heavy with sorrow
And my spirit is weighed down
I wish that I could break free
And leave this sadness behind with a frown
But until it passes, I'll stay here
Lost in this sea of blue
Hoping that someday, somehow
I'll find my way back to you.

*****

30 - THE FAILED POET

I am a failed poet, with a heart full of words,
I struggle to capture the beauty of the world,
My pen spills ink in a desperate attempt,
But the words fall short, my message unkempt.

My verses lack the spark of inspiration,
My rhymes falter with each failed iteration,
I weep in the shadows of the night,
Longing for the power to ignite.

The world is deaf to my silent pleas,
As my poetry falls on unappreciative ears,
My dreams of fame and fortune are dashed,
As my passion for writing is relentlessly thrashed.

But still I write, with a steadfast resolve,
Hoping someday my words will evolve,
Into something more than just scribbles on a page,
A masterpiece that will stand the test of age.

For even a failed poet, with a heart full of pain,
Can find solace in the beauty of the mundane,
And though the world may never know my name,
My poetry will still be a flame.

*****

31 - HAPPINESS

In this moment, pure happiness reigns,
Contentment in my heart, free from all chains.
Worries of tomorrow can patiently wait,
For today, a new beginning, I celebrate.
Embracing the now, in joy I'm sustained.

The sun shines brightly, illuminating my soul,
A world aglow, every part playing its role.
Nature's canvas painted with vibrant hues,
Life's orchestra playing, banishing the blues.
Love surrounds me, a comforting embrace,
In perfect concord, everything falls into place.

Peace engulfs my spirit, serenity profound,
In this moment, happiness knows no bound.
Tranquil waves wash away all cares,
Leaving only serenity, my soul it repairs.
Joy, like a simple tune, fills the air,
A blissful melody, beyond compare.

I find solace in simplicity, life's gentle touch,
A walk in the park, a moment to clutch.
Nature's whispers, a balm for my soul,
A cup of tea, in tranquillity I extol.
The beauty of small things, I cherish so much,
They bring me contentment with their gentle touch.

No need for grandeur or material gain,
I find true happiness in a peaceful domain.
Good mental health, a priceless wealth,
Embracing gratitude, a source of true stealth.
Love of family and friends, a treasure untold,
Their presence in my life, worth more than gold.

Blessed with a shelter, a place to call home,
Nourished by sustenance, no need to roam.
The sun's warm embrace, a comforting ray,
The rhythm of life, a concerto at play.
Gratitude fills my heart, an eternal flame,
For life's blessings, I humbly proclaim.

So, in this grand epoch, I find my delight,
In each passing moment, both dark and bright.
With happiness and contentment, my soul takes flight,
In this epic poem, I revel in life's sweetest height.

*****

I yearn to feel the wind in my hair,
To pedal-power my bike without a care,
But missing ribs make it hard to breathe,
And my dreams of cycling are hard to believe.

I watch as others ride with ease,
Their bodies in motion, their movements a breeze,
But when I try, my lungs won't obey,
And my hopes of cycling slip away.

It's not for lack of strength or desire,
Nor lack of practice, that I cannot aspire,
But missing ribs make it hard to cope,
And my dreams of cycling seem beyond my scope.

I know the thrill that comes with the ride,
The freedom, the power, the rush inside,
But my body won't let me take flight,
And my dreams of cycling remain out of sight.

But even so, I hold onto hope,
That someday I'll find a way to cope,
For the love of cycling burns in my soul,
And I'll keep searching until I reach my goal.

*****

33 - A Gap in Language

In foreign lands, I wander, lost in embrace,
Sounds of unknown tongues, an enigmatic chase.

Words entwined like vines, elusive, out of sight,
I yearn to unravel their mysteries, find solace.

The fragments I grasp, like jewels in my palm,
Each syllable a gem, a moment to embrace.

Yet conversations whirl, a tempest in the breeze,
I strive to keep pace, in this linguistic race.

Fluency, a distant star, shining far above,
I navigate the darkness, seeking its trace.

Imperfect, but resolute, I walk this path,
In pursuit of mastery, with unwavering grace.

The journey unfolds, a symphony of desires,
Through valleys of language, I find my own space.

With each step, I grow, in knowledge I thrive,
A seeker of wisdom, in this foreign place.

Though the road is long, I cherish every stride,
For in each word's embrace, triumph I embrace.

*****

34 - MANNERS

Manners are key,
To being polite and free,
Respect for all,
Makes society stand tall.

*****

35 - HOW TO GET TO THE MOON

To get to the moon, you need a plan
And some wacky ideas, if you can
So put on your helmet, strap in tight
And let's take off into the night

First, you could try to jump real high
And hope you'll land up in the sky
With a little luck and a lot of spring
Maybe you'll end up on that lunar thing

Or maybe you could build a giant slingshot
And launch yourself into the spot
Aim for the moon, with all your might
And hope you'll make it there by night

If that doesn't work, you could try a balloon
Fill it up with helium and let it swoon
Up, up and away, towards the sky
Maybe you'll float to the moon, oh my

Another option is to build a ladder so tall
Climb up it and never fear to fall
Reach the moon in one long climb
And become the first astronaut of your time

Or how about a catapult, with a great big throw
Aim for the moon and let it go
Fly through the air, as well you might
And hope you'll land on the moon that night

If all else fails, you could try to dream
Close your eyes and let your mind gleam
Fly to the moon, in a dream so real
And experience that lunar feel

So, my friend, there are many ways to get there
Wacky ideas, but we must beware
It's not that easy, as you might know
But with imagination, let's give it a go!

*****

Lo! Surreal be the methods to peel an apple,
Whence I conjure the bizarre, strange and supple,
Let me regale thee with awe and wonder afar,
With ways that astound, from realms bizarre.

First, the telekinesis shalt thou wield,
Unleash thy psychic might, thy power unsealed,
Focus thy energy upon the apple's skin,
And behold! The peel floats away, wafting in the wind.

Next, the levitation method, a bewitching sight,
Wand in hand, incantations taking flight,
Lift the apple aloft, in a magical embrace,
As the peel vanishes, disappearing without a trace.

Then, the time warp approach, daring and bold,
Step back in time, where secrets unfold,
To an era ere the apple's life took form,
And peel it afore it breathes, a marvel to perform.

For those fond of melodies, music in their hearts,
Play a harmonica or flute, wherein prowess imparts,
Notes cascade upon the apple's tender rind,
And the peel dances, twirling, leaving none behind.

And lo! Lastly, the alien's otherworldly way,
A ray gun from distant stars, in hand shalt thou sway,
Zap the apple's skin with a cosmic burst,
Behold! The peel disintegrates, swiftly dispersed.

Thus, surreal be these methods, fantastical and grand,
To peel an apple, defying the known land,
But fear not, should these methods be too surreal,
A humble knife shall serve, a simple and trusty ordeal.

*****

When getting dressed, some may find
That bending over is not kind
To backs and knees that feel the strain
And cause discomfort and sometimes pain

But fear not, there's a way to dress
Without causing your body distress
Here's a poem to guide you through
A technique that's simple, tried and true

First, sit down on a sturdy chair
With clothes and shoes within your stare
Slip on your socks with ease and grace
No need to bend down to your lace

Next, put on pants with elastic waist
No buttons or zippers to interlace
Slide them up with gentle ease
Until they rest just below your knees

Then, don a shirt that buttons down
No need to bend to pull it around
Button up from top to bottom
Until your outfit is quite awesome

Last but not least, slip on your shoes
No need to bend, no need to lose
Your balance or your sense of poise
Just slide them on and feel the joys

And there you have it, a way to dress
Without causing your body distress
So, sit right down and take your time
Getting dressed can be just fine.

*****

38 - KISSING

Kissing, an act of affection so pure,
Expressing emotions that words can't ensure.
From gentle to passionate, there are types galore,
Strategies of kissing that one can explore.

There is the peck, soft and chaste,
A quick touch of lips, not a moment to waste.
It's a sweet little kiss, perfect for greetings,
A gentle sign of affection, with no beating.

Then, there's the French, oh so famous,
A tantalising kiss, that's simply outrageous.
Lips locked in a passionate embrace,
Tongues entwined, making hearts race.

The Eskimo is a kiss so cute,
Noses rubbing together, like two lovebirds in cahoots.
It's a gentle way to show affection,
A sign of love and deep connection.

Next, the butterfly, soft and light,
Fluttering eyelashes, a kiss so bright.
It's a delicate touch, with no pressure or force,
A gentle way to show love and remorse.

The lip-biting kiss is playful and a bit riled,
A sign of passion, with a hint of mischief.
It's a kiss that's playful, and never too brief.

Spiderman is a kiss that's unique,
Upside-down, hanging, an embrace so chic.
It's a kiss that's daring, with a hint of danger,
A moment so thrilling, it'll make you a stranger.

Then, there's the earlobe, a kiss so soft,
A gentle caress, that'll take you aloft.
It's a kiss that's intimate, a sign of devotion,
A moment so special, with no commotion.

The neck kiss is divine,
A gentle touch, that'll make you feel fine.
It's a kiss that's sensual, a sign of desire,
A moment so intimate, that'll set hearts on fire.

Kissing, an act of love, so pure and true,
Expressing emotions, that words can't construe.
From gentle to passionate, there are types galore,
Strategies of kissing, that one can explore.

*****

The sun sets low on the horizon,
And I feel a chill in my bones,
As I realise that I am no longer young,
And my age has quickly grown.

I look back on my life,
And reflect on the memories I've made,
The good times and the bad,
And the choices I have weighed.

I see my reflection in the mirror,
And notice lines and wrinkles forming,
My hair has turned grey,
And my body is less performing.

The years have passed by so fast,
And I did not see them go,
I was too busy living my life,
To notice time's flow.

But now I feel the weight of age,
And it's a heavy load to bear,
My energy is not what it was,
And my mind is full of care.

I see the world through older eyes,
And it's a different view indeed,
I have more patience and understanding,
And my desires have receded.

I've learned valuable lessons,
And grown wise with time,
But I also mourn the loss of youth,
And the vigour of my prime.

I wonder where the years have gone,
And if I have lived them well,
And I hope that I have left a mark,
And made some stories to tell.

Now I am in the autumn of my life,
And the leaves are falling fast,
But I'll hold onto my memories,
And cherish them to the last.

I'll embrace my age with grace,
And let my heart be bold,
For even though I'm getting old,
I still have stories to be told.

*****

40 - CRÈME CARAMEL

A pot of milk and sugar doth glow,
Whipped to perfection, with eggs in tow,
A creamy mixture, to chill and grow.

A dish of caramel doth sweetly greet,
As golden syrup, it does complete,
A dessert that's truly hard to beat.

With your silky texture, oh so fine,
Your caramel sauce, rich and divine,
A dessert that's simply worth the time.

As taste and texture blend, it commences,
A perfect harmony of sweet essence,
A dessert that's simply sheer opulence.

This dessert, its beauty is unfurled,
A masterpiece of culinary swirl,
A dessert that's truly a wonder to behold.

Crème Caramel, a dessert that's the most,
A beauty to savour and cherish, utmost,
A dessert that's simply a heavenly host.

*****

41 - An Upside-down Window View

The world is always changing,
a constant state of flux.
Window the out staring,
thoughts wandering in my mind.

The world appears to be upside down,
as if a different reality to find.

The sky below, the ground above,
clouds floating in a sea of blue.
The trees stand tall, roots reaching high,
branches stretched out, a different view.

Birds swim in the air,
fish flying in the sea.

The world is topsy-turvy,
a new perspective for me.
I see the sun and moon collide,
day and night in a constant fight.

Stars shining in the morning light,
a strange and wondrous sight.

In this upside-down world,
my thoughts and worries fade.
I am lost in the beauty,
of this surreal escapade.
But as the world flips right-side up,
and reality returns to me.

I realise that sometimes,
we need to look at things differently.

Staring out of a window,
upside down or right-side up.
The world is always changing,
a constant state of flux.

*****

42 - THE AIR WE BREATHE

The air we breathe, so pure and clean
Is taken for granted, it would seem
We inhale it in without a thought
Never realising the gift we've got

The trees and plants produce the air
And yet we harm them, without a care
We cut them down, pollute the earth
And wonder why our lungs can't find their worth

The air we breathe, it's always there
We don't think about it, it's everywhere
We don't appreciate the breath we take
Until the day our breath we can't make

The smog and fumes, they fill the skies
Our careless actions, we can't disguise
We poison the air, the water, and earth
And yet we wonder what we're worth

The air we breathe, it's vital to life
Without it, we would feel so much strife
It gives us energy, keeps us alive
Yet we take it for granted, we don't strive

To protect it, to keep it clean
We ignore the signs, we're being mean
We think only of ourselves, our wants and needs
And forget that the air, we all do breathe

So let us pause, and take a breath
And remember the air, its life-giving breadth
Let us cherish it, protect it with care
For the air we breathe, it's precious and rare.

*****

Oh, how it hurts when you stub your toe
The pain shoots up and doesn't let go
You hop and dance, tears in your eyes
Wondering how such a small thing could cause such a size
You curse and yell at the offending object
Whether a table, a chair, or a stone subject
You swear you'll move it, never to repeat
But alas, you know it's a promise you won't keep
The toe is nursed and try to forget
The throbbing ache that makes you upset
But the memory lingers, a lesson learned
To watch your step, and be more concerned.

*****

In webs of deceit, they skilfully entwine,
Falsehoods and lies, spreading darkness line by line.
Their poison-tongued words inflict strife and distress.

With practiced ease, they craft tales anew,
Twisting truths to serve their own skewed view.
Their mask conceals, manipulating those who question.

Small or grand, lies deceive the trusting heart,
Hidden behind masks, tearing trust apart.
Consequences bitter, trust's loss hard to mend.

Thriving they continue, hearts dulled, conscience estranged,
Their web of lies spun until their own truth is deranged.
Beware their words, for they aim to bring demise.

Truth, a sharp weapon, piercing through their fears,
Cutting the web of lies, clearing the atmosphere.
Hold firm to the light, for truth always prevails.

Liars may try to pull you down in their deceit,
But truth, reigning supreme, claims victory sweet.
The crown of truth, unyielding, forever it wears.

*****

45 - Fast Growing Grass

Grass grows fast, so very fast,

Springtime rains, and sunbeams cast
Their magic on the earth below,

And soon the green begins to show.
The blades shoot up, they reach so high,
Stretching upwards towards the sky,

A sea of green, a waving tide,
That grows and grows on every side.
It seems to happen overnight,
A transformation to delight,

From barren ground to lush and green,
A wondrous sight to be seen.
The grass grows fast, so very fast,
But soon the summer heat will last,
And then the blades will turn to brown,

As autumn leaves fall to the ground.
But even then, the grass will grow,
Beneath the snow, beneath the cold,
And come the spring, it will emerge,
Once again to take its surge.
So let us marvel at its pace,
This humble grass that fills this space.

*****

In the rolling hills of Bulgaria,
Where the sun shines bright and the air is pure,
Lies a tradition that's been kept alive,
For centuries, without a pause or a strive.

It's the art of making Rakia, the clear brandy,
A beverage so beloved, it's almost candy,
And for those who know its secrets and tricks,
It's a journey that's full of twists and kicks.

It all starts with the harvest of the fruits,
Plums, apricots, quinces, or grapes in boots,
Picked at the peak of their ripeness and sweet,
To ensure that the flavour is hard to beat.

The fruits are then washed and crushed,
Into a pulp that's then mushed and brushed,
And left to ferment in giant barrels,
Till the sugar turns into alcohol, no hassles.

The next step is the distillation process,
Which separates the good from the mess,
A copper still with a long, twisted pipe,
Is the tool that makes Rakia so ripe.

The pulp is heated, and the vapours rise,
And the spirit is distilled till it reaches new highs,
The first and last drops are always discarded,
For they contain impurities that are not regarded.

And when the Rakia starts to flow,
It's a moment that's worth the show,
The clear, colourless liquid that drips,
Is the fruit of labour that never skips.

But Rakia's true beauty lies in its taste,
A delicate balance of sweet and waste,
A smooth, velvety texture that glides,
And a warmth that spreads through the insides.

It's a drink that's meant to be shared,
With friends and family, it's paired,
And with every sip, stories are told,
Of love and laughter, and memories old.

So, if you're ever in Bulgaria,
And want to experience a tradition that's pure,
Look for Rakia, the clear brandy,
And take a sip, it gets you randy.

*****

Spitting in the road, habit so old,
Controversial, seen as crude or bold,
Reflection of culture, ingrained and vast,
Spitting in the road, habit so old.

Expressing disgust, emotions unfold,
Passed through generations, stories told,
Judgment withheld, understanding amassed,
Spitting in the road, habit so old.

Reflection of culture, ingrained and vast.

*****

At the table, one should sit up straight,
With hands on lap, patiently wait,
For the host to signal it's time to eat,
And then begin with a polite greet.

No slouching or hunching, please sit tall,
And if you must cough or sneeze, do it to the wall,
Cover your mouth with a napkin or hand,
So as not to spread germs throughout the land.

Napkins should be placed on lap with care,
To protect clothes from any food that may ensnare,
And should be used to wipe mouth and fingers clean,
But not blown on, crumpled or dropped in between.

When using utensils, start from the outside in,
And don't wave them around like a wild sin,
Hold them with poise, not like a shovel or rake,
And don't lick or suck on them, for God's sake.

When eating soup, it's not a race,
Gently spoon it up at a steady pace,
And don't slurp or gulp it down with a clatter,
Or you'll be sure to create quite the matter.

When drinking, lift the glass with care,
And take small sips, not big gulps to spare,
Don't gulp, slurp or make any loud noise,
And remember, when finished, it goes on the table, not the floor, nor your
toys.

Chew your food with your mouth closed tight,
Don't talk with your mouth full, it's not a sight,
And if you need to get something out of your tooth,
Use a toothpick, not your finger, that's the truth.

If you need to leave the table for a bit,
Say "Excuse me" and wait for a bit,
And when you return, don't cause a stir,
Sit down quietly, like a graceful sir.

When finished, place utensils on plate,
At the six o'clock position, it's not too late,
And push the plate forward, without a sound,
The server can take it away, and your table will be cleaned and found.

Table manners are important, that much is clear,
They show respect and consideration, with cheer,
Remember to use them, and with pride,
And you'll be invited back, with a smile so wide.

*****

49 - MISSED BUS

Heart racing, feet pounding the damn ground,
Chasing after the bloody bus, with a leap and a bound,
Breathless and panting, trying to catch the damn ride,
But alas, the bus pulls away, leaving me to just abide.

Missed it by a hair, a fraction too late,
Left standing on the damn curb, feeling the weight
Of the missed opportunity, the chance that's bloody gone,
As I watch the bus disappear, moving on and on.

But life goes on, as it always bloody will do,
Another bus will come, another chance anew,
So, I take a deep breath, let go of the damn past,
And wait for the next ride, with hope that will bloody last.

*****

50 - WE ALL HATE SUPERMARKETS

In the land of plenty, where abundance reigns,
There's a place we all dread, causing endless pains.
It's the dreaded supermarket, where we all go,
To pick up groceries, a necessary foe.

We hate the long lines and the crowds so dense,
As we push our carts with reluctant suspense.
Endlessly searching for the items we need,
Only to find out they're out of stock indeed.

The fluorescent lights and the sterile aisles,
Are enough to make anyone lose their smiles.
It's a soulless place, devoid of any charm,
Where shopping is a chore, and we mean no harm.

We hate the maze-like layout, so complex,
That makes finding anything a constant vex.
The endless choices that make us confused,
As we stare at shelves, feeling somewhat abused.

The pushy sales tactics and the constant ads,
Are enough to drive us all completely mad.
We long for a simpler time, where we could shop,
Without being bombarded with every marketing prop.

The checkout lines are a test of our patience,
As we stand there, silently praying for cessation.
The beep of the scanner and the rustle of bags,
Are the sounds that make us all start to drag.

We hate the prices, always on the rise,
As we're forced to pay more for the same old supplies.
The constant up-selling and the impulse buys,
Are enough to make us all start to despise.

In the end, we all hate supermarkets, it's true,
For all the reasons mentioned, and even more too.
But we all keep going, out of sheer necessity,
For without them, our cupboards would be empty.

*****

In lines we wait, from dawn 'til dusk, patiently we stand, without a fuss, in crowded streets and shopping malls, we queue for service, obeying calls.

From banks to airports, and theme parks too, our manners show, we've much to do, in orderly lines, we take our place, our turn will come, with grace and grace.

The reasons why, we queue so well, are varied and complex, as you can tell, it's not just manners, or social norms, but efficiency too, and how it forms.

For instance, in a busy store, a queue can make, the shopping chore, much more bearable, and less a fuss, with structure in place, we're less likely to cuss.

In airports too, we wait in line, for boarding passes, or a glass of wine, but in doing so, we're more relaxed, and better prepared, for what's ahead.

And when we queue, we're not alone, for others wait, just like we've shown, and conversations, may be had, with strangers met, who aren't so bad.

In the end, the reason's clear, we queue to show, that we're sincere, in following rules, and playing fair, to those who serve, and show they care.

For lines may form, but they don't last, our turn will come, and soon be past, and so, we wait, with patience true, for in the end, we'll make it through.

*****

52 - LEFT-HANDED PEOPLE

Left-handed people, oh how unique,
Their hands move in a different technique,
In a world made for the right-hand majority,
They navigate with their own dexterity.

From writing to sports, they face a challenge,
Tools designed for righties can be a disadvantage,
But lefties persevere with creativity and skill,
Their left hands moving with an effortless thrill.

Some see lefties as a curious rarity,
But they're just as capable with their dexterity,
Their brains wired in a different way,
A gift that shouldn't be kept at bay.

Left-handed people, oh how they shine,
Their differences make the world more divine,
May we celebrate their talents and gifts,
And embrace their unique left-handedness.

*****

53 - MEN VERSES WOMEN

In the tapestry of existence, two strands entwine,
Men and women, a duality divine.
Through the annals of time, their paths have traced,
Bound by nature's hand, with contrasts interlaced.

Men, like towering oaks, strong and steadfast,
With muscles chiselled, as if from mountains vast.
Their voices resonate, commanding the space,
A symphony of depth, a resonant embrace.
With shoulders broad, they bear the weight,
Of burdens and battles, in life's tumultuous state.

Yet within their core, lies a tender flame,
A vulnerability, sometimes obscured, but never tame.
In quiet moments, their hearts reveal,
The softness and yearning they often conceal.
For beneath the armour, strength tempered with grace,
Lies a wellspring of emotion, a sacred inner space.

Women, like willows, graceful and serene,
Their essence, a dance, ethereal and pristine.
Their voices, a melody, gentle and pure,
A soothing balm, for wounds that endure.
With curves that flow, they embody art,
A tapestry of curves, a masterpiece from the start.

But do not be fooled by their delicate frame,
For within their souls, an inferno aflame.
Their resilience unmatched, an indomitable force,
A depth of courage, an unyielding source.
For beneath the surface, a fierce determination,
An unwavering spirit, that defies limitation.

Together they stand, in harmonious accord,
Each a complement, a completion of the chord.
For where one finds strength, the other finds grace,
An alchemy of energies, that intertwine and embrace.
In their union, a symphony resounds,
The balance of yin and yang, profound.

In these contrasting realms, the world takes shape,
For it is in their union, that life finds escape.
In their differences lies a sacred power,
A yin and yang dance, an eternal shower.
For in this grand tapestry of existence's grace,
Men and women entwine, a celestial embrace.

*****

54 - BBQ Love

Smoke and fire twine,
Flavours divine.
Barbecues, passion's dance.
Streets collide,
Sizzles provide,
Feasts unmatched, advance.
Aprons donned,
Creations spawned.
Flavours fill the air.
Grill's bright stage,
Secrets engage,
Love's fusion, rare.
Tender briskets,
Saucy picks,
Seared steaks impress.
Chicken wings,
Spice that sings,
Ignite the night's caress.
Aromas swirl,
Air's sweet twirl.
Flavours entice.
Gathered kin,
Laughter within,
Memories, a spice.
Kissed delight,
Burgers ignite.
Toppings, pure bliss.
Anticipation grows,
Each bite shows,
Pleasure's fiery kiss.
Vegetal treats,
Smoke's gentle feat.
Nature's bounty graced.

Mushrooms, corn,
Asparagus born,
Barbecue dreams embraced.
Communion found,
Flames surround.
Camaraderie's art.
Novice's quest,
Masters blessed,
Grill's love, a spark.
Primal desire,
Sustenance's choir,
Nature's connection found.
Life's treasure,
Shared pleasure,
Feasting, hearts unbound.
Raise tongs high,
Cheers reach the sky.
Grills aflame, ignite.
Barbecues unite,
Palates excite,
Souls take flight, alight.

*****

55 - BIRDSONG BATTLE

In the realm of melodies that grace the skies,
Birds gather, aiming to please with each trill,
A contest fierce, where avian voices rise.

The Nightingale's song, celestial surprise,
Dulcet notes echo through woods and hills,
In the realm of melodies that grace the skies.

Mockingbird weaves tunes, skilfully applies,
Mimicking others, a virtuoso's skill,
A contest fierce, where avian voices rise.

Skylark soars high, his melody defies,
Touching heavens, hearts with joy it fills,
In the realm of melodies that grace the skies.

Blackbird sings, soulful ballad belies,
A mournful tale his melody distills,
A contest fierce, where avian voices rise.

Warbler warbles, a jewel in disguise,
Delicate notes flutter with nature's frill,
In the realm of melodies that grace the skies.

Thrush's voice commands, resonates and sighs,
Enthralling all with its timbre's thrill,
A contest fierce, where avian voices rise.

Canary's trills, radiant and wise,
A symphony of joy, she does instill,
In the realm of melodies that grace the skies,
A contest fierce, where avian voices rise.

In this chirpy ode with an aviary choir,
Their songs ascend, like flames reaching higher,
A contest fierce, where each voice vies,
In the realm of melodies that grace the skies.

*****

In the vast cosmic sea, galaxies dance,
Harmony echoes in this celestial expanse,
Mere mortals dwell on a speck, so small.

Lost in dreams, ambitions standing tall,
Our minds deemed mighty, yet significance shall fall,
Fleeting chime in the tapestry of space and time.

Look up, behold the heavens' radiant prime,
Stars shining bright, cosmic lights sublime,
Witnessing empires rise and fall, as walls we build.

Boasting knowledge and might, truth unfulfilled,
Wisdom falters against the unknown's test,
Mysteries abound, understanding's quest.

From birth to end, universe's eternal crest,
Grasping at theories, truths we can't divest,
Peering into vast depths, our feeble minds surpassed.

Time measured briefly, the universe's theme so vast,
Woven tapestry of stars, dust swirling fast,
Our arrogance eclipsed by its infinite thrust.

Progress, conquest, fame we tirelessly amass,
Glory sought, names fading like whispers in grass,
Civilizations rise and crumble, sandcastles decay.

Empires built, monuments washed away,
Dust to dust, lost in the haze of time's sway,
Ponder our place, humility must prevail.

Arrogance banished, universe's might unveiled,
Fraction of a fragment, nothingness we embrace,
Marvel at cosmos's wonders, beauty we chase.

In the grand tapestry, solace we find,
Purpose and rhyme, our existence defined,
Speck in cosmic sea, part of the mystery grand.

*****

As youth gives way to age, the body feels the cold,
And warmth that once came easy now seems harder to hold.

The chill creeps in, a shadow on the soul,
As winter grips the heart and takes its toll.

The heat of passion fades, a distant memory,
And in its place, a sense of melancholy.

The fire that once burned bright now flickers low,
As life's relentless winds of change begin to blow.

But in the chill of winter, there is a beauty too,
A stillness in the air, a sense of something new.

For as we age, we gain a different kind of grace,
A wisdom born of years that nothing can replace.

So let the frosty winds blow and the snowflakes fall,
For in the cold of winter, we find our deepest call.

To live each moment fully, to savour every breath,
And find in aging's chill a new lease on life and death.

*****

58 - WHISTLE

Whistle
Echoes
In the
Empty air,
Melody released
From puckered lips,
A soft breath transformed,
Escaping confines of the soul,
Floating, dancing, swirling, soaring,
Carrying secrets, dreams, and desires,
A symphony of sound, pure and untamed,
A language of joy, whimsy, and yearning,
Unleashing freedom, transcending the mundane,
Whistle, dear heart, let your spirit take flight,
Embrace the melody, embrace the light.

*****

In waters deep, a drowning soul I be,
Engulfed in waves, a tragic destiny.
Gasping for air, my lungs with sorrow fill,
As darkness claims me, my spirit grows still.
Beneath the surface, life's grip slips away,
Lost in the abyss, devoid of light.

The ocean's depths, an abyss profound,
A haunting silence, no solace found.
Tossed by currents, despair takes its toll,
My weary heart sinking, losing control.
Engulfed in waves, a tragic destiny,
Gasping for air, my lungs with sorrow fill.

The weight of water, a suffocating grasp,
A cruel symphony, the ocean's solemn rasp.
With every struggle, my strength wanes thin,
Lost in the depths where hope has never been.
Beneath the surface, life's grip slips away,
Drowning, I sink, my hopes begin to fall.

The cold embraces, a watery embrace,
A final resting place, a sombre space.
The whispers of life, fading with each breath,
The ocean's cruel mistress, the bringer of death.
As darkness claims me, my spirit grows still,
Silent screams suppressed, unheard by all.

The depths surround me, a world turned grey,
Surrendering to fate, I sink forever away.
Each stroke of panic, a futile endeavour,
Silent cries for help, lost to the vast endeavour.
The ocean's depths embrace, my heart astray,
A desperate struggle against the water's tether.

In this watery tomb, where dreams decay,
A solemn requiem, as life slips away.
The ebb and flow, a melancholic dance,
A tragic fate, a circumstance of chance.
Silent screams suppressed, unheard by all,
The world above oblivious to my plight.

A mournful dirge, sung by the depths below,
An elegy for a soul lost in the flow.
A symphony of sorrow, forever unheard,
In waters deep, my final song is stirred.
Drowning, I sink, my hopes begin to fall,
Lost in the abyss, devoid of light.

*****

60 - SMELLY FEET

There once was a woman with smelly feet,
Whose odour could surely defeat,
Any nose within range,
It was truly quite strange,
Her shoes seemed to emit pure deceit.

Despite washing them every day,
The smell refused to go away,
So she tried something new,
And it worked, who knew?
She changed her shoes without delay.

Now her feet are much fresher indeed,
And his shoes no longer emit that foul seed,
She can walk with pride,
With no one to chide,
And her friends are grateful indeed.

*****

61 - Autumn's Embrace

Golden leaves drift down
A tapestry of red and brown
Nature's paintbrush, a fleeting crown
Autumn's embrace, a sight to astound

The crisp air bites, a reminder of change
A shifting season, nature's exchange
But in this moment, a moment so strange
A bittersweet beauty that can't be arranged

For soon the cold will creep in
And these colours will fade like a sin
But for now, let us revel in
Autumn's embrace, a wistful win.

*****

62 - ANTS IN YOUR PANTS

There once was a fellow quite vexed,
With ants in his pants, what a text!
They crawled and they tickled,
His movements, they pickled,
Oh, those ants, they sure kept him hexed!

With each step, they danced and they pranced,
Their tiny legs making him danced.
He jumped and he jiggled,
But they just giggled,
Those ants, they were surely entranced!

He tried to sit still, oh, so calm,
But those ants, they just caused him alarm.
They marched and they scurried,
His sanity buried,
Oh, those pants were their antsy charm!

In desperation, he found his way out,
Removed his pants with a shout.
The ants scattered, they fled,
From his legs to his head,
Finally free, no more ants about!

Always remember this tale, my dear friend,
When ants in your pants do descend,
Don't fret or despair,
Just strip if you dare,
And let those pesky ants mend!

*****

63 - PRECIOUS WATER

Majestic falls, cascading with grace,
A symphony of water in nature's embrace.
Mists rise high, dancing in the air,
Enchanting sights that leave hearts aware.
Nature's artwork, beyond compare.

Lakes and ponds, serene and still,
Reflecting the sky with tranquil thrill.
Home to creatures, a thriving domain,
Where life flourishes, in harmony's reign.
A haven of peace, untouched by disdain.

Oh, water, you're a precious treasure,
Sustaining life with boundless measure.
In every form, you bring delight,
A symphony of nature, shining bright.
Your essence, eternal, in day and night.

*****

About the Author

Martin Miller-Yianni is an author who recently made his foray into the world of poetry with his debut collection, "I am Bad at Poems." Born in Erith, Kent in 1958, Martin's early career centred around education, working as a primary school teacher and providing support to learners with specific needs, (dyslexia). However, it was his move to Bulgaria in 2005 that sparked his passion for writing.

Despite lacking formal training, Martin's dedication and versatility as a writer quickly became apparent. After the age of 50, his curiosity about the world and passion for storytelling led him to embark on a writing journey, exploring the power of words to create immersive and meaningful experiences.

While Martin's earlier works primarily focused on non-fiction, delving into subjects that fascinated him, "I am Bad at Poems" marks his first venture into the realm of poetry. Drawing from years of research and personal insights, Martin weaves together a collection that delves into the complexities of human emotions, relationships, and the enigmatic nature of life.

Martin's writing style is characterised by its honesty and detail, inviting readers into a world that is both familiar and extraordinary. His relatable poems feature introspective and thought-provoking narratives, aiming to inspire, entertain, and evoke a deeper understanding of the human experience.

With this book, Martin embarks on a new chapter in his writing as a hobby. Humble and grateful for the opportunity to share his poetry with a wider audience, he hopes that readers will find solace, joy, and inspiration within the pages of his collection. Martin's words aim to resonate long after the final poem is read, leaving a lasting impact on those who engage with his heartfelt expressions.

***